This Faber book belongs to:

_____

'It was good. There were dinosaurs. Can you read it again please, Mama?' Jackson, age 2 ½

'Oooooh.' Asher, age 18 months

'The colours are beautiful, and the dinosaurs are very funny.' Mischa, age 3

'I like singing with the dinosaurs.' Emily, age 3 ½

'I like that one [the Grand Old Duke of York].' Edward, age 2

'It's good for boys and girls. For young ones.' Madeleine, age 7

First published in the UK in 2014 by Faber & Faber Limited
Bloomsbury House, 74–77 Great Russell Street, London WC1B 3DA

Collection copyright © Faber & Faber Limited, 2014
Illustrations copyright © Valentina Mendicino, 2014

HB ISBN 978–0–571–30833–0
PB ISBN 978–0–571–31709–7

10 9 8 7 6 5 4 3 2 1

The moral rights of Valentina Mendicino have been asserted
A CIP record for this book is available from the British Library

FSC
www.fsc.org

MIX
Paper from responsible sources
FSC® C020056

Dinosaur Rhyme Time

Favourite Nursery Rhymes
for Baby and Toddler

Illustrated by
Valentina Mendicino

ff

FABER & FABER

Row, row, row your boat,

Gently down the stream.

Merrily, merrily, merrily, merrily,

Life is but a dream!

Incy wincy spider

Climbed up the water spout.

Down came the rain

And washed the spider out.

Out came the sunshine

And dried up all the rain,

So incy wincy spider

Climbed up the spout again!

The wheels on the bus go round and round,

Round and round,

Round and round.

The wheels on the bus go round and round,

All day long!

Round and round the garden

Like a teddy bear.

One step,

Two steps,

Tickle you under there!

Mary, Mary,

Quite contrary,

How does your garden grow?

With silver bells

And cockle shells

And pretty maids

All in a row.

I'm a little teapot, short and stout!

Here is my handle, here is my spout.

When the kettle's boiling, hear me shout,

Tip me up and pour me out!

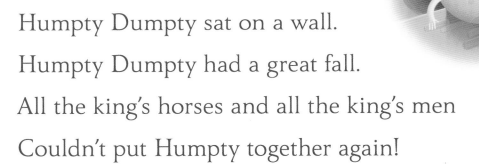

Humpty Dumpty sat on a wall.

Humpty Dumpty had a great fall.

All the king's horses and all the king's men

Couldn't put Humpty together again!

Doctor Foster

Went to Gloucester

In a shower of rain.

He stepped in a puddle

Right up to his middle

And never went there again!

Rain, rain, go away,
Come again another day!

Ring-a-ring o' roses,

A pocket full of posies.

A-tishoo!

A-tishoo!

We all fall down.

Lavender's blue, dilly, dilly,

Lavender's green,

When I am King, dilly, dilly,

You shall be Queen.

If you're happy and you know it,
clap your hands!
If you're happy and you know it,
clap your hands!
If you're happy and you know it,
and you really want to show it,
If you're happy and you know it,
clap your hands!

Oh, the grand old Duke of York,

He had ten thousand men.

He marched them up to the top of the hill,

And he marched them down again!

And when they were up, they were up,

And when they were down, they were down,

And when they were only halfway up,

They were neither up nor down!

One, two, three, four, five,

Once I caught a fish alive!

Six, seven, eight, nine, ten,

Then I threw it back again!

Little Miss Muffet sat on a tuffet,

Eating her curds and whey.

Along came a spider,

Who sat down beside her

And frightened Miss Muffet away!

Jack and Jill went up the hill

To fetch a pail of water.

Jack fell down and broke his crown

And Jill came tumbling after.

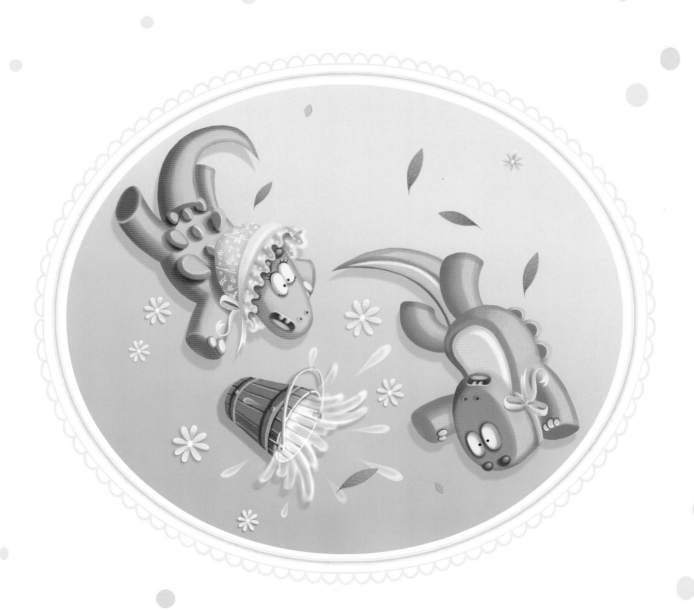

One, *two*, buckle my shoe.

Three, *four*, knock at the door.

Five, *six*, pick up sticks.

Seven, *eight*, lay them straight.

Nine, *ten*, a big fat hen.

Eleven, *twelve*, dig and delve.

Twinkle, twinkle, little star,

    How I wonder what you are,

Up above the world so high,

    Like a diamond in the sky.

Twinkle, twinkle, little star,

    How I wonder what you are.

Rock-a-bye baby, on the treetop,

When the wind blows, the cradle will rock.

When the bough breaks, the cradle will fall

And down will come baby, cradle and all!